Dear Reader,

By purchasing this book you have made a big step towards becoming a Millionaire!

Please note that this book is not a scam at all! You only have to study and practice the following online modules. Please & please use them very wisely because these techniques are very powerful and tested in real life by Jordan Belfort the known as "The Wolf Of Wall Street".

Exactly How To Ethically Persuade Anyone
To Take Any Action. PLUS Increase Your Income, Sales, Closing Rate And Confidence!

HERE'S A SMALL SAMPLE OF WHAT YOU'LL LEARN.
The FOUR core elements of the inner game of sales. (These four elements are absolutely essential to your success. If you lack even one of them, you will end up actually sabotaging your own success!)
How to get into instant rapport with your prospects and how to use that rapport to gather massive intelligence. (Your prospects will be predisposed to trusting you, so they'll tell you what their highest values are and where their pain lies.)
The art and science of Straight Line prospecting. (You'll learn how to develop a multimillion-dollar sales pipeline free of tire-kickers, so never waste time again.)
The four key elements to creating ethical presentations that actually close the deal. (To be blunt, most sales presentations are totally misguided and actually stop you from closing the deal.)
How to instantly squash objections and limiting buying beliefs, turning skeptics into buyers. (This proprietary belief-busting technique is the secret sauce of the Straight Line System, and will empower your clients to make positive buying decisions)
The secret to closing calmly and consistently every single time without even the slightest bit of high pressure. (It's elegant, it's classy, and it's ridiculously effective.)
The ten-step formula for building a never-ending stream of customer referrals and creating customers for life. (You'll make your life a thousand times easier with this proven, paint-by-numbers formula)
How to raise money through Venture Capital and Angel Investors, so you can start using

Other People's Money to fund your ideas and grow your business

The step-by-step process of Straight Line Negotiating, including the seven magic words that allow you to get the lowest price every time)

And, again, this is just the beginning. Once you've been through Jordan's Straight Line Persuasion training, you will be literally unstoppable!

YOUR ONLINE PROGRAM CONSISTS OF:

Module #1:
The 3 Basic Tenets Of Straight Line Persuasion

Module #2:
The Art and Science of Prospecting

Module #3:
Mastering the Art of Tonality

Module #4:
Being A Leader and a Visionary

Module #5:
The Inner Game of Sales

Module #6:
The 5 key Elements of the Straight Line System

Module #7:
The Art and Science of Qualifying

Module #8:

Creating Presentations that Close Anyone Who's Closable

Module #9:

The Art and Science of Looping: how to turn objections into Closes

Module #10:

Creating Customers for Life and Generating Massive Referrals

Module 1: https://www.youtube.com/watch?v=i9OSLjsSntE

Module 2: https://www.youtube.com/watch?v=EDyJ_RlHESc

Module 3: https://www.youtube.com/watch?v=gM-E3aCLT2E

Module 4: https://www.youtube.com/watch?v=-WVTUEYKrgk

Module 5: https://www.youtube.com/watch?v=ZM0AcDZ_Rsw&t=720s

Module 6: https://www.youtube.com/watch?v=keuAkaJqn0k

Module 7: https://www.youtube.com/watch?v=r4gVtvVtXzY

Module 8: https://www.youtube.com/watch?v=8S5ubnHhmXk

Module 9: https://www.youtube.com/watch?v=1VEwp6NELJs

Module 10: https://www.youtube.com/watch?v=-I8kQClCsNk

Home / Book Reviews / Jordon Belfort – Straight Line Persuasion System Notes on "The Wolf Of Wall Street"

Jordon Belfort – Straight Line Persuasion System Notes on "The Wolf Of Wall Street"

By Abhinav Gulyani September 25, 2014 Book Reviews 16 Comments

12

Contents [hide]

- 1 Module 01 – 3 Tenets of Straight Line Persuasion
- 2 Module 02 – Art Of Prospecting, 5 Keys To Sales Mastery
- 3 Module 03 – Mastering Tonality, Capture Attention in 4 Seconds
- 4 Module 04 – Being A Visionary, True Secret To Success
- 5 Module 05 – Inner Game Of Sales, Forces That Create Lasting Results
- 6 Module 06 – The S.L.P. System, Master Formula For Controlling The Sale
- 7 Module 07 – Art Of Qualifying, Asking The Right Questions
- 8 Module 08 – The Presentation, Power Of The Three 10's
- 9 Module 09 – Power Of Language, Cutting Through To The Close
- 10 Module 10 – Becoming A Person Of Influence, Create Customers For Life
    -
        - 10.0.1 Share this:
        - 10.0.2 Related

Jordon Belfort is one of the main leading character played by Leonardo DiCaprio in the movie "The Wolf of Wall Sreet". The real Jordon Belfort in real life is a motivational speaker, an author & is also having his famous "The Straight Line Persuasion System" Training & Coaching Program which is retailed at 1999$ bucks.

I was intriguad & skeptic about his Sales System developed by him, which has been used by everyone who wants to better understand sales & marketing psychology. I have been going through the course since past week and have been utilizing my time by creating notes of the whole series of videos which his coaching program included in the package.

Here's the note & review for the system made by yours truly. At the end of this post you will also find an option to download the PDF of this same notes:

Download this article in PDF

Please support us, use one of the buttons below to unlock the content.

tweet

like

+1 us

MODULE 01 – 3 TENETS OF STRAIGHT LINE PERSUASION

- o Persuading is about allowing people to overcome the obstacles that prevent them from taking action they should be taking
- Beliefs
- Fear

- **Persuading is empowering people**
  - o Straight Line Selling is Goal Orientated Selling
  - o It's to get people to buy things they should buy

- Everyone have limiting beliefs from making decisions

  o The key to selling is to maintain the control of the sale

3 Keys To Success In Sales

  o Desire to be really wealthy
- Why do you want this

  o Take advantage of an opportunity when it knocks on your door
  o A commitment to work your ass off
  o Persuading is about allowing people to overcome the obstacles that prevent them from taking action they should be taking
- Beliefs

- Fear

- **Persuading is empowering people**
  o Straight Line Selling is Goal Orientated Selling
  o It's to get people to buy things they should buy
- Everyone have limiting beliefs from making decisions

  o The key to selling is to maintain the control of the sale

3 Keys To Success In Sales

  o Desire to be really wealthy
- Why do you want this

  o Take advantage of an opportunity when it knocks on your door
  o A commitment to work your ass off
  o Closing Model
  o Consultative Selling
  o These models are bullshit but you should be closing from the start
  o There is nothing wrong with influencing people
  o For the next 60 days embrace this system & stretch and work twice as hard
  o *There are windows that open for a short time and when they do work twice as hard*
  o Do not pressure a client to do something they should not do
  o Do not pressure a client to do something they should not buy

The Straight Line System
- It's Goal Orientated Selling vs Random Conversations
- You have to look at the end result first which is to close and make money

3 Tenants Of The Straight Line System
- ***Develop Instant Rapport***
  – Both conscious & unconscious
  – It's not small talk
  – **It's about them recognising that you care and are an expert and can help them achieve their goals**
  – It never ends

- ***Gather Intelligence***
  – There are specific questions you need to ask
  – You need to listen a lot more than talk

- ***Controlling the sale by keeping it on the straight line***
  – The straight line is the perfect sale but they will try to get you off the line
  – You need to keep them as close to the line and when you are off the line you do only two things:
  – Develop rapport
  – Gather intelligence
  – You must control the line

THE 4 "MUSTS" OF MASTERING THE STRAIGHT LINE SYSTEM
1) Set your goals just above what you think is possible and make them bigger and brighter

2) Use Positive Think Language Patterns
  – Self talk
  – The first person you must sell is you

3) Find your "WHY"

4) Shed all programming that sales is evil

Examples of Great Persuaders
- Bill Gates
- Warren Buffet
- Oprah Winfrey

Key Points
- **You must vanquish your fear of failing or looking stupid in the process.**
- **Sometimes you have to look foolish in the name of progress.**
- There is no embarrassment in struggling – the embarrassment is in quitting
- All people care about is how much heart you have when you do something
- Never blame externally – look and examine why internally
- We do this because of fear and it stops us from moving forward

- The only thing that stops you from getting what you want in life is the bullshit story you tell yourself why you can't
- **be honest with yourself**

3 Things To Take Advantage Of An Opportunity
- Where you are
- Where you want to go
- How to get there

2 Types of People
- Those who get everything in life
- The influencers

- The other 95% that don't
- Creature of circumstance

- You should see things as they are not worse than what they are

- Instead see them better than they are and go for that

At this point he states you might be sceptical because you are now consciously incompetent

2 Actions
- What are your "why's?"
- What would you do with the money?

MODULE 02 – ART OF PROSPECTING, 5 KEYS TO SALES MASTERY

- Prospecting is not just about finding people who are interested in buying your product or service, but about weeding out the people who are not interested or who don't qualify.
- Looking for the nugget

- Never try and turn non buyers into buyers

4 Archetypes
- There are people who are ready
- Great group

- People not quite ready and still shopping
- Good group

- People who are curious
- Not good

- People who could be dragged and still won't buy
- Not good

- You need to qualify people quickly
- You must use a script

The Art of Sifting
- You MUST be quick, elegant, and non-alienating.
- You MUST use a script.

- Keep your powder dry
- Keep your best stuff until you need it

- People have inner blocks and beliefs to buying

The action threshold
- Is an unconscious set point past which the person will take action
- It's the sum of all the good things
- It's the sum of all the negative things
- Limiting beliefs
- People run movies on the negatives and positives of buying
- **The Action Threshold is the unconscious set point that somebody has to be motivated to in order to take action.**

The Sales Funnel
- Work backwards from how much you want to hear
- If you want to make $200,000
- Thats $4k a week which is 2 sales

- That is 6 pitches

- That needs 8 appointment

- That needs 40 calls with the decision maker – connects

- That needs 24 dials per day

- The only thing you can control for sure is the dials

First Impression
- You have only 4 seconds on the phone to communicate
- **Enthusiastic as hell**
- **Sharp as a tack**
- **A figure of authority**
- This shows you a person who can give them control of their lives and help them achieve their goals
- $1/24^{th}$ of second in person and you will be judged
- The way you are dressed

- The way you carry yourself

    o People will make a mental picture of you on the phone

Trust
- o Certainty
- o Clarity
- o Conviction
- o Courage
- o Confidence
- o This is what people want
- o You want to be perceived instantly as an authority figure

The Lot Chart
- o I want to earn £1,000,000
- o I need

MODULE 03 – MASTERING TONALITY, CAPTURE ATTENTION IN 4 SECONDS

- o Tonality is the hidden part of persuasion because it speaks to someone on an emotional level
- o It helps develop rapport on an unconscious level

FIRST SCRIPT: You have 4 seconds …
- o Hi, is John there?
- o Hi, John! This is , calling from Global Capital, in Tampa, Florida. How's it going today?
- o Great! Now, if you recall, you attended a seminar last Thursday night over at the Marriott Hotel, with one of our top Forex traders, James Arnell. Does that ring a bell?

OPENING SCRIPT DISTINCTIONS
- o It must capture the friend to friend tone
- o While you are listening and watching the exercise on the video, pay attention and take note of the following tonal distinctions:

1) **Use up-tones to pace and lead.**

2) Raise your voice at the end of "Global Capital, in Tampa, Florida" to infer a **micro-agreement.**

– *If you say it low it communicates that you don't care*

– By raising your voice it communicates – *"right you recall don't you?"*
– They will then go to remember it

3) Use a **tone of "mystery"** at "Now if you recalL"
– *Now they try and recall*
– *Narrow your eyes when you do this*

4) How's-it-going-today **(contracted)** says, "I really want to know!"

5) The **power of the pause,** not before "at the Marriott Hotel."

6) **Five beats is the "kill zone" of the pause** in the script.
– *Withoneofour – said as one word*
– *Group words together and stand others out*

7) **Raise your tone** to say, "Does that ring a bell?"

8) The words, "One of our top traders" are **grouped/said together.**

9) Use **hypnotic patterns.**

SECOND SCRIPT: And one last chance

- Charisma is about tonality
- Okay, great. Well, the reason for the call today is that you're one of the last of the group who hasn't actually enrolled yet, and if you have sixty . seconds, I'd like to share an idea with you. You got a minute?

CLOSING SCRIPT DISTINCTIONS

- While listening to and watching the exercise on the video, take note of the following tonal distinctions:

1) **Use transition words**: Well, now, and but.

– *Ok great* – enthusiastic

2) **Slight drop in tone** at "Well, the reason for the call" implies you have a secret **and scarcity**.

3) Emphasize that it's scarce; that there's not a lot around. Your tone must be congruent with this!

4) Use transition words to go up and down in tone and volume.

5) **Whisper** and they'll see you as **someone worth listening to**-especially coupled with**"bottled enthusiasm."**

6) Your "bottled enthusiasm" is rooted in absolute certainty; it's still there when your tone drops, and the prospect knows it.

7) "Got a minute?", stresses the **"reasonable guy."**

8) **Building rapport is in your tone.**

MODULE 04 – BEING A VISIONARY, TRUE SECRET TO SUCCESS

- People will buy into your vision but not your goals
- Turn your should into will and must
- How you see yourself in your own mind is your disassociation and then you associate yourself with that vision

The 3 Musts Of Closing

1) The client has to love your product.

2) The client has to love and trust you.

3) The client has to love and trust your company.

- Your state affects your prospect

Use needs to establish:

- Airtight an emotional case
- Airtight logical case
- Make sure they feel like they made a great decision
- Imply that you care with your tone

Body Language

- When you are talking to a woman you stand directly in front of her 2.5 feet
- When you are talking to a man you stand at an angle
- No pinkie rings
- No goaties
- Use a normal handshake
- A wimpy hand shake is that they are trying to show power out of you

- Always dress well
- Solid Suit – slight pink colour with white shirt
- 72% of the time you must make eye contact
- Mirroring

- Powerful unconscious rapport

MODULE 05 – INNER GAME OF SALES, FORCES THAT CREATE LASTING RESULTS

- o Be willing to do today what people are unwilling to do so you can have the future you want
- o Be prepared to do what it takes

Identifying Old Patterns

- o Eliminate the word should
- o Change the word problems to challenges
- o Stop letting past mistakes control your current thinking
- Your past is your greatest assets

5 Ways To Overcome Obstacles

1. Getting rid of old patterns.

2. Mastering your emotional states.

3. Understanding how the brain works.

4. Mastering your fear.

5. Setting lofty goals.

5 Keys For Setting Effective Goals

1. Write down your goal.

2. Put a date on it.

3. Identify the people, groups and organizations you need to align with.

4. Take massive action.

5. Identify what's working, what isn't, and change your approach accordingly.

MODULE 06 – THE S.L.P. SYSTEM, MASTER FORMULA FOR CONTROLLING THE SALE

The 3 Musts Of Closing

1) The client has to love your product.

2) The client has to love and trust you.

3) The client has to love and trust your company.

- o Once these 3 things align then you ask for the order

The Way To Ask Questions

- o Ask in an off handed way
- – Out of curiosity, what are you trading right now?

- o Always apply money aside with tonality not with words
- o Let me ask you a question – does the idea make sense to you
- – High end tone

- o Developing rapport is not talking about the guys life
- – Would an expert spend his time talking trivial?

- – You need to find out can he afford it and does he need it?

- o Never interrupt someone talking
- – Oh right, I'm actually form the countryside, by the way….

- – Tonality

- Use tonality to imply that you care
- Use tonality to show that you are interested in his life
- Demonstrate that you time is valuable
- Use your body language

Presentation

- Transition after you ask the last qualifying question
- **Based on everything you told me this is a perfect fit for you**
- The sale starts when they say no
- Anticipate objections
- Knock out their buying beliefs on the way
- When you knock out a belief they drop straight away

- You are constantly trying to find out their buying beliefs

To get through the buying beliefs:

- **Create an Airtight logical case**
- It must be better than sliced bread

- **Create an Airtight an emotional case**
- **Crack through all their limiting beliefs**
- Do not give them the great stuff up front, leave it until last
- Make sure they feel like they made a great decision
- Imply that you care with your tone
- You must get all 3 of these down
- If they still don't buy it's either money or a belief
- Keep looping until you knock them all out
- Finish with the intelligence
- Start broad and get specific

MODULE 07 – ART OF QUALIFYING, ASKING THE RIGHT QUESTIONS

The Actual Questions

1. Identify The Client's "Why"

2. Memorize Questions In Order

3. Ask Permission To Ask Questions

Transitions
- o Just a couple of quick questions so I don't waste your time
- – Tonality is here to help

- – So high

- o Just a couple of quick questions so I can better serve you
- o Tonality should be:
- – I care,

- – Trustworthy

- – I have your best interests at heart

- o *Future pace with results in advance*

BIG PICTURE QUESTIONS

1. **1. What did you like/dislike with it?**
– This identifies the client's likes and dislikes, which will be used later on to customize your pitch to meet the client's specific needs.

– Typically applies to a product that they have used before

– People pay more for customisation

1. **2. What would you change or improve with your current source?**
– Ask what your client would change about their current situation.

1. **3. What's your biggest headache with**
– This uncovers the emotional problems he/she might be experiencing.

– Pay close attention to the answer. You will use this information later in your pitch.

1. **What's your ultimate objective?**
   - Once you understand your client's goals and objectives, you can become the right person for the job.

1. **What would be your ideal program?**
   - Ask the client to be as specific as possible in terms of the product or program.

SPECIFIC QUESTIONS

1. **Of all the factors, what's most important to you?**
   - What factors are most important to your client?

   - What is he ultimately trying to accomplish with you?

1. **Have I asked about every detail that's important to you?**
   - Is there anything your client might have missed?

   - Does he have any additional concerns or questions for you?

   - JB doesn't like this question

WAYS TO KEEP YOUR POWDER DRY!

1) **Do not narrate the client's answers.**
   - Leave out any comments, including those that demonstrate your active listening.

   - You don't want the client to feel relaxed just yet.

   - Let him talk himself into feeling a little uneasy.

2) **"Feel the client's pain."**
   - Let the client know that you understand his specific gripes.

   - Explain that you care about his answers and will do everything you can to help him reach his goals.

3) **Listen!**
   - Salespeople love to talk. This is not the time for it.

   - Listen at least twice as much as you talk.

- What you're doing is identifying your client's emotional wants and physical needs.

ASK INVASIVE QUESTIONS

- o Ask the client how long they have been thinking about refinancing their home, trading some stock, buying a car-whatever it is you are trying to sell.
- o This question could potentially elicit a cache of information, so listen carefully.
- o **HOW LONG HAVE YOU BEEN _____ ?**
- "How long have you been thinking about buying a Porsche?"
- "How long have you been thinking about this piece of equipment?"
- "How long have you been wanting to get into the trading business?"

- o **Say it high**
- o It is important to convey the message that you care about your client and his specific situation. Keep this in mind throughout your questioning.
- o **Other invasive questions:**
- "How much money do you have in the stock market, just a ball park?"
- Say in a nonchalant way
- Use hand language to back off
- "How much do you owe on your mortgage right now?"
- "How far are you behind on your credit cards?"

When you ask these questions, remember two things:

1) Each question has its own tonality. (HINT: Minimize it.)

2) Identify a gesture that supports each tonality.
- **ONCE YOU'VE QUALIFIED YOUR POTENTIAL CLIENT, YOU WILL HAVE ESTABLISHED:**
- *Your product is right for him.* **OR** *He can afford it.*
- **If you cannot fulfill both criteria, do not continue your pitch.**

Transition to the Presentation

- "Well, Based On Everything You Just Told Me, It Sounds Like This Is A Perfect Fit For You."

THE PRESENTATION

- Now it's time for you to go into the main body of your presentation and it's going to be short.
- Here are some components for the basic structure of your pitch. Be sure to use a script when you do this.

1) In the beginning, a script is a work in progress

2) The body should be no more than a page

3) Each word is crucial, so read it back to yourself 100 times

4) Paint a picture, using comparisons and metaphors

5) Link your good or service to a trustworthy figure

6) Create urgency in the last paragraph

7) Go into a soft close, ending with: sound fair enough?

8) There are three responses, and he's not expecting to buy

- Now, after the pitch, the first thing you'll do is expect your first "no."
- Embrace it internally and tonally …

Use Deflection!

- When you hear "no" for the first time, engage in a process called "deflection." Put the client's concern off to the side. Use the exact language pattern below so you can go back and get him to a "10" in his love of your product.
- **LANGUAGE PATTERN #1**

– "I hear what you are saying, but let me ask you a question.

– Does the idea make sense to you?"

- Don't say that you understand what the client is saying. Instead, say you *hear* what he is saying.
- Also, don't say "Money aside, does it make sense to you?" The "money aside" should be implicit in your tonality.

QUESTION #1 Þ LOOP #1

Looping

- After you deflect the client's initial refusal, do not directly ask why he is refusing.
- Instead, go backward on the line and resell your product.
- Your second pitch will be more powerful and bullet-oriented.

– Use the better stuff next

- Use the exact words:
- **LANGUAGE PATTERN #2**

– "And let me say this. The true beauty of the program is … "

EXAMPLE #1
Mistake: You ask, "What kind of work are you doing now and how's it going for you?"
Solution: Never ask a two-part question. Ask the first part and let the client talk. Then ask the second part as a way of keeping the conversation on track. Beware of open-ended questions like "How's it going for you?" These can lead to long, lengthy "memoirs" from the client.

EXAMPLE #2
Mistake: The client talks at length about how he loves to hunt and than asks if you like hunting. You politely say no.
Solution: Even if you hate hunting, do NOT say so! Instead say something like, "I would love to try it someday." Or, "Once when I was a kid, but I just don't have the time these days."
Remember-the client needs to feel like you are just like him.

EXAMPLE #3
Mistake: You ask, "Are you currently invested in the market right now?" but the client has already answered this question earlier in the conversation.
Solution: Do not ask questions that imply that you are reading from a script. That's a quick way to lose business!

EXAMPLE #4
Mistake: You ask, "Just for suitability purposes, how would you say your current financial situation is right now?"
Solution: When asking questions, try not to come across as the Grand Inquisitor. Instead, make it sound like it's no big deal.

QUICK REVIEW:
Try making a sad face, which will help your tone sound more empathetic.

Remember, you are just like them!

Imply that you are there to help the client. Therefore, any answers to such an invasive question will be used for his own good.

THREE DIFFERENT RESPONSES TO ANY QUESTION

1) **"Things really suck right now."**
   – Don't get stuck in the script and respond with "Okay, great…"

   – Take this opportunity to MATCH or ELEVATE his state.

   – For example, "Things could be worse" or "I hear you … "

   – Remember to convey that you care!

   – Don't bring the client out of feeling his pain just yet. Think of it as tough love.

   – **YOU ARE JUST LIKE THEM!**

2) **"Things are not that great. I'm behind on some of my bills."**
   – Again, respond with a bit of an elevated tone.

   – "I totally understand. That's exactly why I called you … "

   – Do NOT say "Oh man, that's awful!" because you will sound disingenuous.

3) **"Things are going well"**
   – Depending on how upbeat the client's tone is, try to match it and elevate it to your tonality.

   – If he sounds only slightly optimistic, try saying, "Well, you seem to be doing better than most folks."

   – If he sounds more upbeat, respond with, "Great, good for you!"

   o A *few tips when asking about money* ….
   – Always keep a disarming tone.

   – Have a "It's no big deal" attitude.

   – Be CASUAL!

MODULE 08 – THE PRESENTATION, POWER OF THE THREE 10'S

Important Tonalities

- o Scarcity/secret
- o Certainty
- o Disarming
- – Create a disarming story

- – It's no big deal

Basic Structure of a Pitch

1) In the beginning, a script is a work in progress

2) The body should be no more than a page

3) Each word is crucial, so read it back to yourself 100 times

4) Paint a picture, using comparisons and metaphors

5) Link your good or service to a trustworthy figure

6) Create urgency in the last paragraph

7) Go into a soft close, ending with: sound fair enough?

8) There are three responses, and he's not expecting to buy

- o Now, after the pitch, the first thing you'll do is expect your first "no."
- o Embrace it internally and tonally …

The Power of Presupposition

- o "You'll make money with it"
- – Please! Give me a break –You'll make money with it

- It's obvious

- Embrace the power of no

Loop #1

Step #1

- Product is fantastic
  - Must be the best thing since sliced bread

- Deflect objections
  - "I hear what you are saying, but let me ask you a question.
  - Does the idea make sense to you?"
  - Do you like the idea?

- Pace-Pace-Lead
  - Match him at his energy level and then slowly raise the energy
  - It's sounds good
  - Exactly!
  - Let me says this – the beauty of this is….

- Listen twice as much as you speak
- Run specific patterns
- End with a great future picture
  - When you have the house you will X

Step #2

- Sell yourself
- Make a metaphor that he has to answer yes to
  - If he says maybe – get certain

  - C'mon if I did x,y & z you wouldn't have

- "Let's cut to the heart of the matter. You don't know me and you don't trust me, so let's deal with that." Tell him about yourself
- Let me re-introduce myself to you
- My name is X, I am the CEO, I have been at this for 14 years and we rely on referrals

Step #3
- Sell your company
- Convey it's a company you can trust
- Then say "do this" – ask for the order

Loop #2
Step #1
- Deflect again
- "Listen I hear what you're saying" and then go back into the looping process again.
- Start reselling yourself and your company, and this time bring out all your heavy artillery.
- Tailor it to the objection and acknowledge it
- Tailor your close to the objection
- "Believe me, all I ask is when you make the first $4,000, go buy your wife a little present because I am sure she deserves it. Sound fair enough?" Then stop talking.
- The first person who talks loses.

One of the most powerful closes is to ask what is the worst that can happen.
- For example, "Let's say you sign up for this program and I am totally wrong and the product doesn't meet your needs. Is the cost of the product going to put you in the poorhouse?" When the client says "no," start building a powerful future pace case.
- Create a picture in his mind of massive benefits from doing business with you.

- *Enjoying the home with your family*
- This interrupts his decision-making strategy and minimizes all the damage he may be thinking about if the product doesn't work out.

- It also effectively boxes the client in because you undermine his two cornerstone buying beliefs: "I don't buy from people and companies I don't know and trust, and I don't buy unless the risk/reward ratio is heavily weighted in my favor."
- The client will never say this to you, but that's what he is thinking.

- Asking, "What's the worst that could go wrong?" disrupts his pattern of thinking and inserts a new one that lowers his threshold for buying.
- If the client says they have to speak with their partner or accountant, go back into another loop.
- Say, "Listen, I understand you have to speak to your partner, but the beauty of this program is .. ," and then position it as the sort of decision they don't need to talk to their partner about. Then loop back into reselling yourself and your company, with each loop getting progressively tighter.

MODULE 09 – POWER OF LANGUAGE, CUTTING THROUGH TO THE CLOSE

1) **Power words such as minimizers, justifiers and reframers.** These are short, simple words and phrases that have a powerful ability to persuade, influence and motivate people.

2) **Offsetting language patterns.** These are used to respond to objections and defuse underlying beliefs that get in the way of closing the sale.

3) **Language patterns for looping.** Looping in essential part of the Straight Line System that involves going backward on the line to resell the client on you, the product and your company. It uses specific language patterns to move the client closer to the sale.

4) **Closing tonal patterns.** The closer you get to closing the sale, the more important it becomes to use the right tonality.

Trigger Words

1) *Virtually.*
- "Virtually" allows you to make bold claims without speaking in absolutes.
- It also protects you from a legal standpoint.
- For example, you wouldn't tell a client, "All my clients make money." One, the client wouldn't believe you. Two, it isn't true. "Virtually all my clients make money" is far more believable and legally defensible. Use "virtually" to avoid speaking in absolutes.

2) *Only.*
- Only is a great minimizer, especially when associated with price.
- When you ask for an order and include a dollar amount, use "only."

- "It's only $49.95" sounds a lot more reasonable than "It costs $49.95."

- Use "only" when mentioning price and asking for commitments.

- *Use this when talking about price*

3) **Because.**

- "Because" is a justifier.

- It provides a reason that causes people to think differently about what you're asking for.

- Use "because" when you need to justify what you're asking for and why you need it.

- Example is the Cialdini copy machine

- *Use this when asking for a commitment*

4) **Cash Outlay/Investment.**

- "Cash outlay" or "Investment" are re-framers.

- It gets the client to look at the cost of the product in a different way.

- For example, "My product doesn't cost anything.

- It's a cash out lay."

- Or (combining two trigger words), "It's a cash outlay only."

- *Apples versus Oranges*

5) **I Would Be Glad To.**

- This re-framer is especially powerful for after the fact.

- Suppose a customer calls you with a question.

- You can say 'I don't know. I'll have to go look that up."

- Or you can say, *"I'm not sure about that. I would be glad to research it for you."*
- "I would be glad to" is a huge rapport builder.

- It also changes how you feel about yourself through the use of positive self-talk.

Offsetting Language Patterns
- These go in at the end of the presentation

1) *Hold your hand every step of the way.*
- Clients always worry that once they buy, you will leave them hung out to dry. This phrase removes that fear and knocks off a huge negative that always exists in the client's mind.

2) *Show you the ins and outs.*
- This works especially well with complex products or services. Many times, people hesitate to buy because they fear they won't know how to use it properly or that it will be difficult to use.

- This pattern offsets that fear by stating that you will show them how to make it simple, easy and wonderful.

3) *Huge upside with little downside.*
- People always worry about what will go wrong if they buy.

- This phrase addresses that fear by convincing clients they have a lot to gain and little to lose by buying your product.

- Of course, it needs to be supported with evidence.

- But this phrase is so powerful it should be used several times during your close.

- *Repeat this one*

4) *Incredibly easy to get started.*
- 'It's incredibly simple' people don't want to expend energy.

- They want to be told how easy it is to modify their loan or to fix their credit. You're knocking out a negative, adding a positive.

5) *In-depth training program.*
- This is a great pattern to use when your product requires people to learn something in order to use it.

- It tells clients that you will be there holding their hand every step of the way.

6) *It's a long-term relationship.*
– This pattern uses future pacing to remind clients what you can do for them over the long term.

– It tells clients that once they complete the transaction, it is just the first step in all the things you can do to make their lives better.

– *This assumes that the first transaction goes well*

7) *It's surefire, paint-by-numbers.*
– You have a system. <u>People love buying systems</u>.
– They especially love turn key systems that are paint by numbers, step by step, move by move.

– Money rolls in, freedom rolls out.

Powerful Closing Patterns

1) *Believe me.*
– "Believe me, if you do even half as well as the rest of the people who have gone through this program you're going to be very, very impressed.

– All I ask is after you've made money with this I want a ton of referrals.

– Sound fair enough?"

2) *Your wife.*
– "Your wife will be kissing you when you walk through the door."

– This pattern knocks out the fear that loved ones will disapprove of the buying decision.

3) *Kid's schools.*
– "If you do this you'll be sending your kids to the finest schools."

– This is a powerful emotional pattern.

– Do not make statements like this if your product cannot live up to it.

4) *I am not getting rich here.*

– This is very effective for getting referrals and building long-term relationships because it insinuates that you're not making any money on the transaction.

– "I'm not getting rich here but I know you're going to do really well with our program and you'll give me a ton of referrals and that's how my business grows. Sound fair enough?

SAVE YOUR MOST POWERFUL LANGUAGE PATTERNS FOR THE FINAL CLOSE!
These include patterns like:

1) If you do even half as well as the rest of the people that have gone through this program ...

2) All I ask if that you give me one shot. ..

– I promise you will be eevry very impressed

3) The only problem you'll have is I didn't call you six months ago and get you started then.

4) Believe me you will not be sorry. Sound fair enough?

Lopping Language Patterns
1) *Does it make sense to you?*
– Tonality is essential. Ask in a calm, curious tone, "Does the idea make sense to you? Do you like the idea?" This is not a pattern to use with certainty.

2) *True beauty.*
– "You see, the true beauty of the program is that it's .... " and then go on to describe how it will solve the client's problems and make his life better. This a beautiful transition and powerful deflection pattern.

3) *If I had been ...*
– "If I had been your financial advisor for the past three years, making you money on a consistent basis, you wouldn't be saying 'Let me think it over' right now. You would probably be saying, 'Let's get started.'" Again, tonality is key.

4) *As far as my company goes ...*
– This is an excellent transition from selling you to selling your company. "I pride myself on doing this.
– **I pride myself** on doing that. I plan on being the top producer in my company.

- I am not going to get there without my clients giving me tons of referrals because they love me.

- And as far as my company goes … " Then go on to say all the great things about your company.

5) *What we can do for you besides this one transaction …*
- This should be presented more as a statement than a question.

- Find three things (which can include your up-sells) you can do for the client outside this transaction. In fact, this pattern is a good way to pre-frame your up sells as benefits.

6) *What's the worst that could possibly happen?*
- This is the ultimate minimizer.

- It allows the client to run through all the possible bad outcomes if the product doesn't work out and compare them to all the positives if it does.

7) *We can start off small.*
- This is an effective pattern for minimizing some of the client's fears while setting the groundwork for doing more business in the future.

- Starting out small does not mean lowering price, although it can mean buying less so that the customer doesn't pay as much.

8) *Please don't misconstrue my enthusiasm for pressure.*
- Today's clients are very distrustful of high-pressure salespeople.

- This pattern allows you to put it out there and defuse it. The client will respect you for saying it. If you don't say it, he may feel you are pressuring him.

9) *I understand what you're saying.*
- This is a great response to the person that says, "Let me think about it."

- It is also a great tool for demonstrating caring and empathy.

- Say, "I understand what you're saying" and then loop back to selling your client on you and the company.

- If the client still wants to think about it after several loops, get a little stronger with your tonality.

- Say, "I understand what you're saying but let me say this there are 3 things ion our business, every factor is in your favour … " and start using some closing patterns.

- *Use scarcity & urgency*

10) **Getting started is very simple.**

- "Getting started is very simple.

- It's just a question of I some basic information."

- This is an excellent soft or trial close.

11) *Cash outlay of only …*

- "Cash outlay" always sounds better than "costs."

- You can also use the term "investment.

Tonality for Closing

1) **If you do half as well…**
- Total certainty

2) **You're going to be very very impressed**
- Utter Sincerity

3) **Sound fair enough**
- Reasonable man

MODULE 10 – BECOMING A PERSON OF INFLUENCE, CREATE CUSTOMERS FOR LIFE

Dealing With Stalls

- If the client truly cannot afford your product, you have to respect it. But never accept a stall. If the client doesn't like the product, loop back and convince him with (with logic) that it is the greatest thing since sliced bread. If the client doesn't trust you or your company, loop back and educate him (with emotion) about how trustworthy you are and how great your company is.
- If a client says your product isn't that good, don't get defensive and don't challenge him. Adopt a tonality of calmness and disarming, and say, "Let me say this. The true beauty of my product is what you haven't found out yet." This tells the client, "You're a smart person. I just haven't given you all the facts yet."
- If the client doesn't like you or your company, say, "Let me tell you a little bit more about my company …. " Then launch into your pitch about how great the owner of the company is, and all the good things he does in the community, etc.

Common objections include:

1) I can't afford it.

2) There's been a death in the family.

3) I need to check with my accountant.

4) I'd like to but it's bad timing right now.

5) I want to check it out.

6) I've been burned before.

7) My wife will kill me.

8) I want to see it first.

9) I need to do more research

10) And of course, the #1 objection: I need to think it over.

Creating a Customer For Life

1) Never duck a phone call.

− All it takes is one ducked phone call to kill the relationship.

- If you have bad news, give it to the client.

- They'll forgive you.

- If you make a bad move operationally or in marketing, act quickly and they'll forgive you.

- If you let the problem fester, they will do business with anybody but you.

2) *Send them to your competitor.*
- If you really can't help your client, tell them where they can get the product they need.

- They will rave about you to their friends and associates.

- More importantly, the next time they need anything similar, they will call you thinking, "If he doesn't have it, he'll know where I can get it."

- This is a powerful strategy that also makes you feel good about yourself.

3) *Remember their family.*
- After you close the client, find out who they are.

- As you're filling out the paperwork, find out if they have kids, when their birthday is, and what some of their interests are.

4) *Use gifts (correctly).*
- Give gifts that the client will actually appreciate.

- For example, don't give hockey tickets to someone who has no interest in the sport.

- Find out what makes your client feel alive outside of work and fill that need with your gift.

- If your client loves fishing, send them a hunting and fishing magazine every month.

- For just $12.00, he will remember you every month for an entire year.

5) *Write effective thank you notes.*
- "Thanks for the gift, it was great" doesn't cut it.

- Get personal and specific.

- Tell the person why you liked it, using emotional trigger words.

- For example, "I absolutely adore the gift you sent me. It looks beautiful sitting on the centerpiece of my table for Thanksgiving."

- "My family were commenting on it"

Motivation
- o Act as if you are wealthy already
- o Act as if you have all the answers
- o Act as if you are super confident
- o ***Every human being can succeed if they only do three things:***
- Harness the basic motivating principles of pain and pleasure.

- Learn to move through fear toward where they want to go.

- Stop focusing on what is wrong with their lives and focus on where they want to go.

www.ingramcontent.com/pod-product-compliance
Lightning Source LLC
Chambersburg PA
CBHW082223220526
45470CB00010B/3291